MW00648411

Don't Hold their Poop A small book about cleaning up life's BIG messes
C.J. Hathaway

Ignite Ambition Publishing

C.J. Hathaway, MAS, MFT
Don't Hold Their Poop
A small book about cleaning up life's big messes

All Rights Reserved

Phoenix, AZ
Igniteambitionlc@gmail.com

Book Layout: Ignite Ambition Publishing
Front Cover Graphics and Book Layout Design: Brenna L. Lundy
Edited by: Cerri Boehm

Printed in PRC
Don't Hold Their Poop-1st Ed.
ISBN: 9780578734705
Library of Congress Control Number: 2020914849

Note to Reader:

You're probably wondering if you can use the contents of a book called "Don't Hold Their Poop"

to make all of your serious life decisions including medical, emotional, spiritually, etc.

Unfortunately, I have to tell you this is not the case. While this book contains thoughts and ideas

of the Writer who has a Masters of Advanced Study, Marriage and Family Therapy, this book is

not to be used for medical, physical, emotional or financial purposes. Use this book at minimum

for a good toilet sesh read and maximum to help you recognize the areas in your life that need to

be cleaned up!

.Hathaway

Contents:

Pop a Squat and Relax

stion, Would you ever rub someone's poop all over yourself? Pretty gross, right? But seriously,
ld you ever, willingly, let some-one hand you their feces and then proceed to rub it on your
y? Most people in their right minds, not those who have some sort of poop fetish of course,
ld probably scream, "Heck no!" to this question. They would probably also ask if I'm a lunatic
sking this question in the first place.

reason that I ask that question is the reason for this book. I am here to tell you the unfortunate
that you are most likely doing this every day if not a few times a week. I am also here to help
understand that this is not occurring in the literal sense but in the emotional sense.

he end of this book, I hope you realize the scenarios where you are allowing people to hand
their emotional poo, how you are "spreading it onto yourself," but more importantly, how to
I it back or "flush" it away. I am also going to help you recognize when you're the defecating
ndant and need a GUT CHECK of your own.

how to use this book...

Before we get into understanding how dung is being dumped on you, I think that it is important to understand how to use this book.

Oops Poops: You will be inundated with information that will help you relate to the content given. These examples are what I like to call, "Oops Poops." These are common times when we allow other people to hand us their emotional poo. These short examples are here to help you recognize similar scenarios in your life.

Bathroom Break

Bathroom Breaks: In effort to connect the examples given to your own life we will often take what I like to call, "Bathroom Breaks". These are areas for self-reflection. Use this time to take a step back to analyze a recent scenario, relive the moment, and dissect what went down.

Dropping a deuce: These areas will define terminology and theories in more detail. This book is not meant to be long-winded, so use this area to gain more insight on concepts and terms.

Dropping A Deuce

Please Wipe Here: Areas for you to take notes to remember concepts or to later reference.

Okay, so now you know how to use this book. Let's stir up some shit.

Lesson 1
Stank On Ya

...p.: Cambridge Dictionary defines poop as, " solid waste from the human body." (Cambridge Dictionary, 2020) As most ...ple are aware poop contains waste products that are being eliminated from the body. Sometimes this includes bacteria, ...igested and digested food particles, salt, corn etc.

... as I mentioned we are not talking about poop in the literal sense. In this book we define poop as, " the negative messages, ...ments, actions or lack thereof, shame and judgement that we have digested throughout our lives." These interactions ...n become broken records in our heads that contribute to how we present ourselves to the world and how we perceive the ...ld views us. This type of poop affects us personally by creating insecurities and shame and skews how we interact ...erpersonally.

... often approach social conflict or disagreements without the understanding that we are not only interacting with that ...son in the moment, but we are also interacting with their defenses and insecurities that were created by negative wasteful ...ssages that person heard and felt throughout their life. In turn, they are interacting with our defenses and internal wounds ...well. The majority of us, usually, do not have the wherewithal of understanding that the other person is in a wounded ego ...tressed head space. We are clueless that our interaction with them has triggered an uncomfortable and sometimes auto-...ic response relating to their past.

Rather we see the conflict as an attack. We begin internalizing or "digesting" the spew that is being projected or "handed" by the other person. We often take it personally, and more times than not, engage in a reactive way ourselves. We yell bac DM back, put down, act aggressively, act passive aggressively. We feel shame, guilt, anger, sadness.

Once the argument is through, we replay it over and over in our heads throughout the day, grumbling up the same emotions we felt during the argument which then activates stronger emotions in that moment

We blame the other person for us feeling like crap all day. Worst of all, we let these feelings build and bu until WE spew our shi$$y feelings all over the place!

It is similar to when you have to go number 2 really bad and when you do, you feel some relief but then realize that you've clogged the toilet.

It's frustrating and it stinks!

Dropping A Deuce

Passive Aggressive behavior: Indirect behavior.

Examples: behavior might include avoiding direct or clear communication, making "beating around the bush" statements, blaming others, playing the victim, sarcasm about their feelings and the situation, backhanded compliments, and hiding anger.

Aggressive behavior: Hostile Behavior
Examples: Verbal hostility, physical aggression, threatening, bullying, name-calling, shouting, and all out brawling.

Passive Behavior: Avoiding Behaviors
Example: Avoiding conflict altogether, not sharing your inner thoughts, feelings, or opinions, lack of assertion, being overly agreeable, or shutting down completely.

When we recognize a person's reaction to us does not match the intensity of the situation prior to the onset of the conflict, we open our minds up to the first sign that the person is in their poop. When we come to the realization that handing of the poop is commencing, we are better equipped to not take the situation personally and set an emotional and/or internal boundary which we will get to later.

Now the good part. This book has been laid out to easily help you understand how to navigate these stinky situations. First you will learn how to "flush" these situations away so that you are no longer taking people's sh#t. Secondly, you will recognize how you are handing your own crap out to the people in your life.

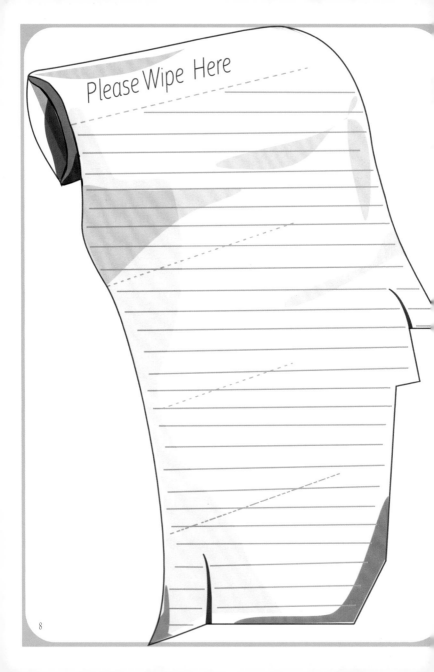

Please Wipe Here

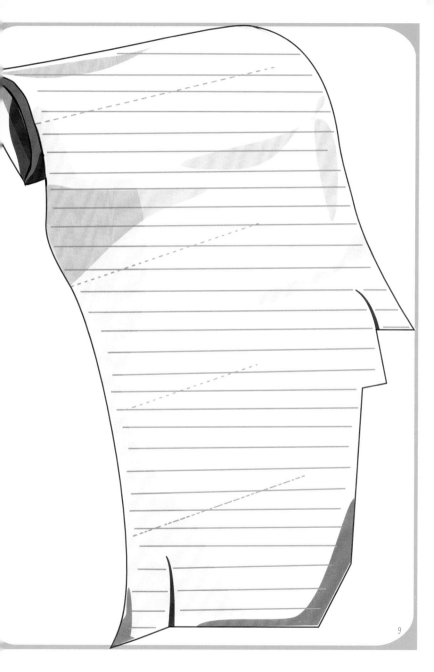

Lesson 2: Today was a Poop Day

I have a second question from my initial,
"Would you ever rub someone's poop all over yourself?"
This one is a little easier, "Do you feel like poop today?" Let me ask that in a different way,
"Are you feeling frustrated, angry, sad, shameful, or regretful?" Have you in the recent past?
If you answered yes, do you understand WHY you are or were feeling that way?
Can you look back on that day and recognize the situation or stimulus that contributed to these feelings?

Recognize that I said, "contributed" to these feelings. Through this book you will learn that every feeling we have is our CHOICE to feel and that no person can MAKE us feel any type of way, but we will get to that a little later.

Stimulating scenarios can look like something like this:

- Your Boss walks into your office and begins scolding you for a project being late when *they* actually failed to provide you with an appropriate timeline

- Your spouse comes home and starts complaining that he or she is so hungry and wish there was food on the table

- You have a customer who continually criticizes your work even though you are consistently helping them.

- You post something on Facebook and a troll begins to body shame, political shame, Mom shame, etc.

Bathroom Break

If you realize your crummy feelings stemmed from an interaction with another person I want you to use this bathroom break to go back to that interaction and remember it as best you can.

Take 3-5 minutes to reflect and list the following:

1. What thoughts were you having in that moment? _____

_____

_____

a. About yourself? _____

_____

b. About the other person? _____

_____

2. What emotions were you feeling? _____

_____

3. What emotions stayed with you throughout the day? _____

_____

4. Did you replay the scenario another time in your day? Did feelings arise when replaying the argument? _____

_____

_____

ow that you have been able to break down the situation including what you were
eling and thinking, can you recognize where you "allowed" the handing of the
oop?

o you recognize how you took the other person's message and YOU allowed it to
rn into a negative thought cycle and/or crappy feelings that lasted throughout
ur day?

his my friend is you holding their poop. So now that you know you are willing to
old another poops, let's chat about, O.P.P. Other. People's. Poop.

Lesson 3: Don't be down with OPP: Other People's Poop

Here's a recent Oops Poop that I was on the crappy end of.

Oops Poops!

I had been working with a family, a father, mother, and daughter for over a ye[...]
The daughter presented with an eating disord[...]
and was seeking therapy with m[...]
As our time together went on, the girls eatin[...]
disorder became worse. Myself and the treatment tea[...]
urged her parents to make significant changes to her routi[...]
but unfortunately her parents didn't liste[...]

This continued for months and progress was limite[...]
because of the parents lack of follow through. I set up[...]
session with the family to discuss their inconsistency. Aft[...]
discussing my concerns in a professional manner, the Moth[...]
reacted by berating me, yelling at me, questioning m[...]
experience and level of expertis[...]

Her Husband then followed suit and t[...]
session turned into a full blown attack. Questions lik[...]
"well how long have you been doing therapy?" and " Do you even know what you'[...]
talking about" were spewing out of their mouths. Their ton[...]
posture, and facial expressions all pointed to this being a full blown attac[...]

So how did I react

Dropping A Deuce

Common reactions could be:

I could have started to feel inadequate as a Clinician. The rush of "I am not good enough" (a common thought I've experienced) could have taken over my body. I could have felt my shoulders tense up and my heart sink into my gut. I could have felt my blood boil and then have exploded on this family and gave them a piece of my mind.

. I could have had a similar experience as #1 but this time instead, allowed shame to boil over. This in turn could have caused me to be overly agreeable and passive in the scenario. I then could have gone home and allowed myself to go into a full blown shame spiral.

I could have been passive aggressive, avoided the conflict by changing the subject and not using my voice. Without expressing my feelings, my frustration, insecurities, anger, would only sit in my body for the rest of the day.

. Name another way I could have reacted based on your past:

_____

_____

_____

_____

_____

_____

Being that I am the Author of this book hopefully you expected me to act in a responsible way. Let me break it down for you:

Instantly I recognized the parents were working within their defense mechanisms because of overwhelming emotions.

I noticed VERY quickly that taking an "I'm better than you" stance was the Mother's defense based on her questioning my ability to treat her daughter. I also recognized the Father's "agree with my wife, don't cause anymore conflict" defense.

So as I am noticing these defenses what I am also doing at the same time is recognizing my own physical and emotional response. I'm not going to lie, I initially felt my adrenaline increase, but for me that is a tell tale sign that I've been triggered. Once I recognized this I reminded myself that this was their poop and it was not for me to hold. I acknowledged the parents feelings while also setting a clear boundary that I would not continue in the session if they were going to proceed in a disrespectful manner. This helped defuse the situation and we were able to proceed forward.

So how was I able to do this? Or more importantly, how can you do this in the future?

You need to learn to F.L.U.S.H. the poop away.

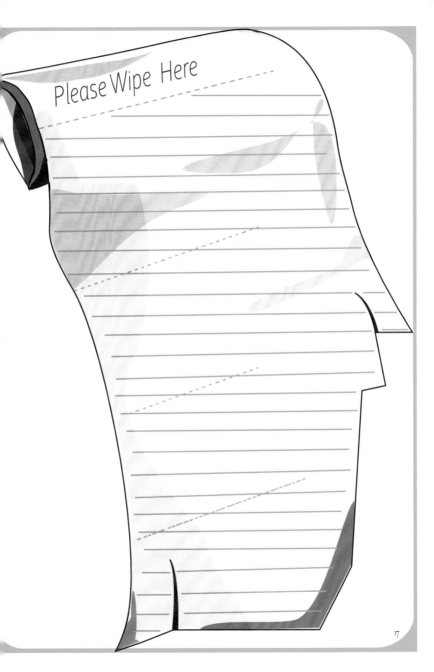

Please Wipe Here

Lesson 4:
I don't FLUSH with YOU.

This lesson is one of the most important of this book. You are about to learn how to recognize when someone is attempting to hand you their poop, how to avoid the internal rumble, how to create blockage, and how to not spread the specimen after the fact. How?

You F.L.U.S.H it away:

1. Face the Situation
2. Listen to my body and thoughts
3. Understand my emotions
4. Set a boundary
5. Handle myself

So let's break each one of these down!

ace the situation: The handing of the poop

'hen finding yourself in an "Oops Poops" scenario you must first, face the tuation for what it ACTUALLY is. During conflict, we get in our heads and art becoming defensive and start forming come-backs to say to the other rson. We become completely clueless to what is actually going on. What e really need to do is look at the facts, stay present, and gather data to help decide how to proceed forward.

how do we do that? Focus on what happened. What occurred prior to the rson popping off at you? Ask yourself this, is this person's response a mmon response to what has occurred? Or are they acting, overly sensitive, notional, reactive, or dramatic? Are they being downright nasty? If their sponse does not "fit" the situation, you can hand them a wet wipe because e handing of the poop has commenced.

Listen to you: The Rumble Within

You are probably thinking, why would I listen to my thoughts when this other person is losing their mind? Welp, a reminder that taking someone's poop requires you to internalize THEY'RE projected thoughts and feelings. When we start to listen to ourselves two things happen.

1. You begin to hear your own words and how this interaction is affecting you.

2. You get to begin to separate yourself from the other person's spew.

If you can begin recognizing these thoughts now, you will be better able to recognize them in the moment. When we listen to ourselves, we begin to recognize the beginning of our reaction to the other person and we gain more insight into ourselves within the situation. Speaking of insight, let's talk about emotions.

What are common thoughts that you have when in a conflict with someone else?

A reminder to think about different scenarios including:

- Direct conflict where you got into an argument face to face
- Social media conflict where someone negatively commented on your post
- An argument over the phone
- When you're in the shower preparing for an argument that hasn't happened, lol!

Write those common thoughts here:

_____

_____

_____

_____

_____

_____

_____

_____

_____

_____

_____

Understanding your emotions: The Heartburn

While negative thoughts can just be "words", the thought usually then initiates an emotion. Words are just words until we put a feeling behind them. One person's response to a disagreement can be very different from another's.

The emotion is what makes us feel crappy. More importantly, as mentioned above, there is a physical response that comes along with every emotion. Tightness in the chest, racing heart, muscle tension, lump in throat, heightened body temperature, shaking, turning red, hot flashes, etc. These are all common physical responses when we are feeling certain emotions.

Dropping A Deuce

Common emotions

Anger	Surprise
Fear	Anticipation
Sadness	Trust
Disgust	Joy
Shame	Contentment
Guilt	

Bathroom Break

What happens to you when you are feeling angry? Sad? Scared? Shame? Guilt?

What occurs in your body when you feel a certain emotion?

Write that down here.

Emotion: _____   Physical Sensation: _____

_____   _____

_____   _____

Emotion: _____   Physical Sensation: _____

_____   _____

_____   _____

_____   _____

Emotion: _____   Physical Sensation: _____

_____   _____

_____   _____

Once you are able to recognize your thoughts and emotional patterns you can recognize how you are or were **figuratively** reaching your hands over to grab that poo.

As a reminder that you are the only person who is in control of both your thoughts and feelings so this is where you take that control back.

Now that you are the master of poopy disaster, you are now able to create some blockage, a set a boundary.

23

Set a Boundary: The Blockage

So before we discuss how, let's talk about what boundaries are. We have two types
boundaries, internal and external.

An internal boundary is the boundary that we need to set with ourselves when we'r
all up in our negative headspace. An internal boundary is necessary when you are in
full blown sh*t spiral in your head. In the simplest terms you are telling **yourself** to
stop.

An external boundary is a boundary that you set with another person. An external
boundary needs to be put in place when someone is acting in a way that makes
you feel uncomfortable. An external boundary can take place in 3 ways, verbally,
emotionally, and/or physically. And in the simplest terms, you are telling the **perso**
to stop.

Both internal and external boundaries help you regulate your system and bring you
back to a comfortable place.

w let's talk about how we make this happen. As I mentioned above, both internal and external boundaries are ply saying "Stop!" But how?

ou go through the FLU of the FLUSH, you will begin to recognize the thoughts in your brain and the emotions feel. These are clear indicators of what internal boundary you need in the moment.

e example is If you are in a shame spiral, talking down to yourself, calling yourself names, then you need to yell)P! This is not my poop! Then you need to replace the negative thinking with a more positive message. "This is my poop, it is theirs, I will not take it." or " I am trying my best" or " I have a right to take space."

r than creating a new message in your brain, you can also start the self regulating process. You can take a deep th(s), you can focus on your breath, you can count to 10, get some cold water, etc.

Easy Self-Regulation skills:

- Square breathing 4 second inhale, 4 second hold, 4 second exhale, 4 second hold

- Start listing things you are grateful for

- Think of your pet (as long as its not an a-hole)

- Tap each finger to your thumb on both hands

- Drink some cold water

- Go for a walk

- My fave, hold some ice in your hand. When your hand is cold AF, its hard to feel anything else

The whole idea behind an internal boundary is to calm your shit down. By using affirmatic and/or self regulating skills, you can create some internal blockage (the good kind, not th need stool softener kind).

Keep in mind you may have to set an internal boundary while at the same time needing to s external boundary.

If you look back at the previous bathroom break on page #21 you listed common thoughts that you have when in conflict.

I want you to now write down positive messages that you can say to yourself in the moment to create an internal boundary.

Bathroom Break

Common Negative Thought:

_____

_____

New Positive Thought:

_____

Common Negative Thought:

_____

New Positive Thought:

_____

Common Negative Thought:

_____

New Positive Thought:

_____

_____

...xternal boundary is, as mentioned above, using your voice, creating space, or saying "No!" or "Stop!" to ...her person.

...break this down:

...bal boundary IS NOT telling someone to STFU or aggressively yelling at someone to STOP! If you are ...g either, you too have lost control of your bowels. Rather when we are asking someone to stop doing some-...that is offending us we must do it in an assertive manner.

...n we use an assertive voice we are saying, "I am maintaining my cool while also asking you to cut your ...out." or "I am maintaining my respect and self control while also asking you to stop engaging with me ...is way."

Dropping A Deuce

Assertive Behavior: Characteristics of assertive behavior include openly expressing your feelings, using your voice, setting boundaries, remaining calm and present

Assertive behavior is when we can openly and honestly express our feelings about a a interaction while still remaining respectful to the other person

Examples of boundaries:

Your Boss walks into your office and begins scolding you for a project being late when **they** actually failed to provide you with an appropriate timeline.

Internal Boundary: "*I have completed the task on time as I was directed*"

External Boundary: " *I understand that this is an important project. The timeline I was given was x based on the email sent, enter date. I believe I met the expectations you set for me.*"

Your spouse comes home and starts complaining that he or she is so hungry and wish there was food on the table

Internal Boundary: "*HE/She must have had a long day, this is not about me or my characteristics as a partner.*"

External Boundary: "*How was your day today? Do you want to talk about it? Oh and dinner will be ready in 30 minutes. Maybe grab something small?*"

You have a customer who continually criticizes your work even though you are consistently helping them.

Internal Boundary: " *I am doing my best to help this customer.*"

External Boundary: "*I feel like I am providing you with great service. Is there another reason you are unsatisfied?*" (put it back on them! Insecure people hate to be called out)

You post something on Facebook and a troll begins to body shame, political shame, Mom shame, etc.

Internal Boundary: " *the people who actually know me think I am great.*"

External Boundary: Block them.

Your job, again, is to stay calm while facing the situation. This may seem unnatural to you but in time it will become second nature.

hat happens if the toilet gets clogged?

he poop handler continues treating you unfairly, you can remind them of the boundary a second
ie. If they STILL continue their spew, you can kindly change the subject, leave the situation, and/or
: a physical boundary i.e, take space, start a conversation with someone else, ask for a time-out.

Bathroom Break Use your original Bathroom Break (Page 12) and write down an internal
boundary you could have given yourself and an external boundary you
could have given the poop handler.

Internal Boundary _____

_____

_____

External Boundary _____

_____

_____

ay now that you've handled the situation, it's time to make sure your sh$t don't stank.

H: Handle myself: Stop the spread

This is the step when you get it all out to feel the most relief. When using the "FLUSH" method the first steps help you to recognize and remove poo. This step, however, makes sure that you're not spreading the poo that was being handed to you.

If we think about the whole concept in literal terms as if someone ACTUALLY handed you their poop, you'd most likely have it on your hands. Then moving through your day every thing that you'd touch you'd leave a little bit of that poo behind.This could be a surface or an individual. Therefore, not only did you accept someone's poop, hold it, and spread onto yourself, you then proceeded to spread it everywhere you went. Not a great image but I need you to put it into perspective to understand this next part.

The "handle yourself" in the figurative sense is making sure that even if you've blocked yourself from being shit on, that you're not then going through your day complaining about it, reliving it, bringing it up, or worse allowing negative thoughts and emotions to bubble up again.

Handling yourself means this, if you have taken all of the steps that are listed above; you were present, you managed your thoughts and feelings, and you've set a boundary your final step is to let it all go.

Now, if you need a moment to process the residual "skid marks" after a confrontation, I understand that. What this means is give yourself 5 minutes to process your emotions, use some more self-regulation skills, and then move on with your day.

Don't bring it up afterwards.

This may sound cr-ASS but everytime you bring up the incident, you relive the thoughts and feelings that you experienced. This in turn affects how you show up for yourself and others in your life. So if you allow yourself to let go and not relive or "spread" the poo everywhere, you show up in your life so fresh and so clean!

So that is how you FLUSH away poop that has been handed to you. Initially you may only be able to conquer F and L portions of the tool. Then the U, S, and H. Don't worry about this! Practice makes perfect! Use this tool often and eventually it will become second nature and the phrase, "That's not my poop" will be just as common as "thank you and you're welcome."

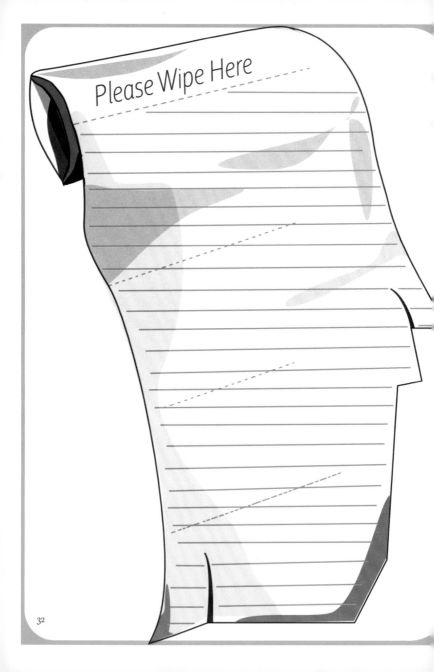

Please Wipe Here

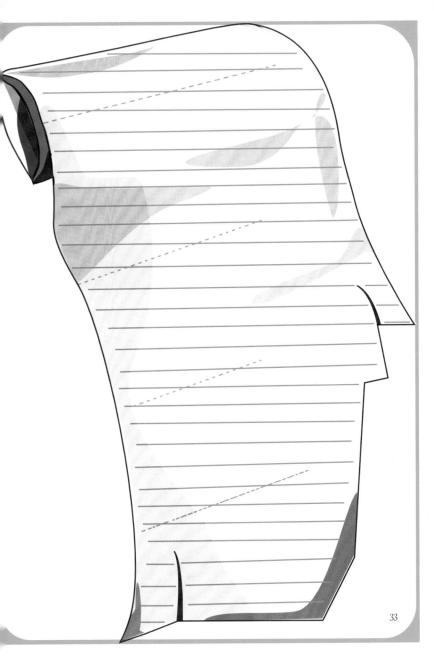

Lesson 5: Gut check yourself before you wreck yourself!

So we've talked a lot about gaining awareness when another person is attempting to hand us their poop but we haven't discussed how to recognize when we are the fecal offender.

Oops Poops!

I recently made a mistake planning a flight for my Husbands birthday. I didn't recognize the mistake until 36 hours later, which was outside of the cancellation timeframe. I thought to myself, it's 12 hours after the cut off to make a change which was 24 hours after booking. I was sure someone could help me with this. So I called the customer service line only to be greeted by a Bot rather than a person. The Bot, of course, had difficulty hearing my response and I had to repeat myself multiple times, slowly getting more frustrated each time I answered.

After my battle with the Bot, I then got someone on the line. Because I was already annoyed, I felt instantly annoyed by the Customer Service Representative and started the conversation with an attitude. I explained the situation only to be told that there was NOTHING they could do.

My annoyance was through the roof. This is where I engaged in a GUT CHECK.

G.U.T. C.H.E.C.K.

1. Get a hold of yourself
2. Uncover your thoughts and emotions
3. Take a moment, chill

4. Confess
5. How were you hurtful
6. Explain your negative impact
7. Commit to not doing it again
8. Karma, make it right

Get a hold of the situation:

This is most likely going to be the hardest part of this step, especially if you're deep in your scat. As I've mentioned before YOU are the only person who can stop yourself from splattering your mess everywhere. Checking yourself when you're popping off at your spouse, child, or the poor Gal at Star bucks, will give you your first sign that you are in the process of dung devastation.

Bathroom Break

This is going to be a long bathroom break as will we continually add to reliving this scenario. Grab the air freshener!

Think about the last time you lost control of your "bowels" and attempted to hand your Poo to someone else.

Write down the following:

What was the environment or stimulus? _____

_____

_____

_____

What did you feel physically? _____

_____

_____

_____

What actions did you take? _____

_____

_____

_____

_____

What was the other person's involvement or lack thereof?

_____

_____

_____

_____

Uncover your Thoughts and Emotions:

Once you grasp a hold of the situation, you then need to check into your thoughts and feelings. Are you tense, anxious, fearful, annoyed, or angry? Reference the common emotions DAD on page #22. Has your physical state of being changed? Are you tense, hot, shaking?

Are you having thoughts of blaming or shaming the other person? Thoughts that they are doing something to you on purpose? Thoughts of, "How dare they treat me this way?"

Bathroom Break

Continued...

What emotions did you feel in the moment? _____

_____

_____

_____

What thoughts did you have? _____

_____

_____

_____

Again, it is SO important to understand your internal process, especially when you're the caca culprit. When you self reflect, you stop the pattern created by your emotional brain, and you connect with the logical side of the brain. This in turn helps you recognize if you're overreacting or to put it more kindly, your reaction is not in lin with the situation. This can then help you with the next part of your GUT CHECK, take a moment.

Take a Moment, Chill.

Now in social situations you can do several things to help you "soothe your stomach" if you will. You can simply take a calming, deep breath. You can take a cold drink of water. You can leave the room and collect yourself in the restroom. You can take a walk.

All of the same self-reflection tools we used in FLUSH can be applied here as you GUT CHECK. Your responsibility in that moment is to calm yourself down. REMEMBER, you are the ONLY person who can control your thoughts and feelings. As much as you want to blame others for how you feel, in all reality you are choosing to feel in any way that you feel. Taking a moment, gives you back responsibility and power to change the moment. So relax, dude.

Okay so now that you've taken care of yourself, it's now time for you to hold yourself accountable.

CHECK is the portion of the tool where you not only apologize for your behaviors but take further responsibility to how your actions affected the relationship and environment.

Confess

First things first, you confess your wrong doing. This sounds like "I am sorr
for taking my anger out on you" or "I apologize for losing my sh*t" or "Th
is totally not your fault and I should not yell at you." This shows that you ha
recognized that you started flinging your feces and you'd like to clean up th
situation.

Bathroom Break Continued...

How could you have confessed to your behaviors in the previous bathroom break?

_____

_____

_____

_____

_____

_____

_____

How were you hurtful?

Secondly, express how you were hurtful. This sounds like "I feel terrible for treating you this way" or "I feel guilty for having lost control." This is NOT where you go off telling the person why you lost control or where you offer a big BUT. The BIG BUT takes away from you being responsible for your actions. If the person is close to you and later wants to discuss what's going on, that's fine, but it needs to occur outside of this discussion. Expressing how you were hurtful shows empathy for the other person's feelings related to your behavior.

Continued...

Bathroom Break

In the above scenario, how could you have explained how your actions were hurtful, disrespectful, or downright nasty?

_____

_____

_____

_____

_____

_____

_____

_____

Explain how your actions affected the situation:

The third step is to explain how your actions negatively affected the situation. This sounds like "Now, I've held up your line and people are waiting" or "I recognize my crap could affect your trust in me." This shows the other person that you understand not only what you are apologizing for, which you acknowledged in confessing your wrong doing, but why it was wrong and potentially affected your relationship.

Bathroom Break Continued...

Are your legs asleep yet? How did you actions negatively affect the situation?

_____

_____

_____

_____

_____

_____

_____

Commit to Not Doing it Again!

The fourth step to your CHECK, is to commit to not doing it again. This can be done with both people close to you and those you do not know, like the gal at Starbucks. It sounds like "I will not continue to speak to you like this" or "I promise to not speak to you this way again." This commitment should be something that you can, ahem, commit to. So no need to be an over-achiever here, make it simple and realistic.

Bathroom Break Continued...

How could you have committed to the person you pooped on?

Bathroom Break it down here:

_____

_____

_____

_____

_____

_____

Karma

Lastly is Karma. Make it right. Give the person a hug, if you ask and they allow. Give them a nice tip, smile, high-five, do a kind gesture whatever it is. Remember that karma is real and you don't want to feel her wrath. You can make it right with the other person but also YOURSELF. Don't beat yourself up. Find grace in the fact that you recognized the moment before it got too wild. Making it right is not only going to help ease the situation but it will also make you FEEL better.

I hope that by GUT CHECKing yourself, you too can handle the stinky situations you create and offer a more delightful and pleasant you.

Now if you're wondering if my GUT CHECK in my Personal Oops Pops situation helped me get what I needed done, I'm sorry to say it did not. However, the Customer Service Rep trie to help me for over forty-five minutes contacting the airline and attempting everything sh could to change the flight. I thanked her profusely and was truly grateful for her help.

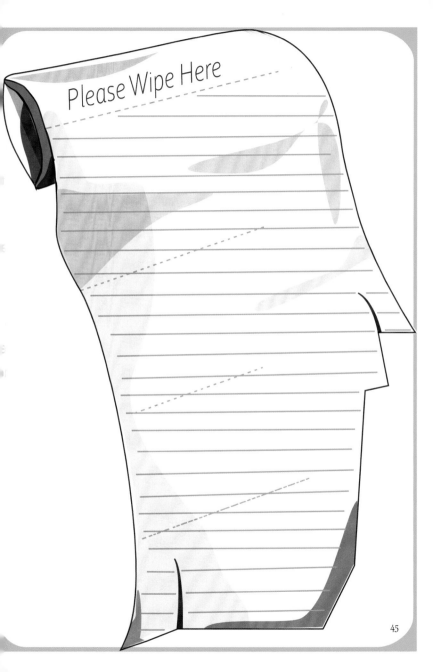

Please Wipe Here

45

Rear End

So that's it, you have now learned how to handle the stinky situations that you encounter in your life. A reminder that the lessons given in this book are just that, lessons. I do not expect you to master these tools right away, so find some comfort in the process of learning and strengthening these skills.

If you find your toilet continually clogged, come back to this book a second, third, seventeenth time. If you realize, or are told by a loved one, that you continue with your own stool struggles, don't sweat, GUT CHECK.

Just always remember this, YOU are in charge of your own thoughts and emotions. You now can recognize how you ALLOW others booty booze to bother you. So while I fully allow you to tell someone, "That's not my poop, it's your poop!", I also expect you to not be salty but rather soothe and be emotionally responsible. I hope to also encourage you to continually check into your internal experience to keep yourself regular!

From this point forward I want you to find relief for Number ONE, you, while avoiding someone else's Number TWO.

Keep it clean, my friends.

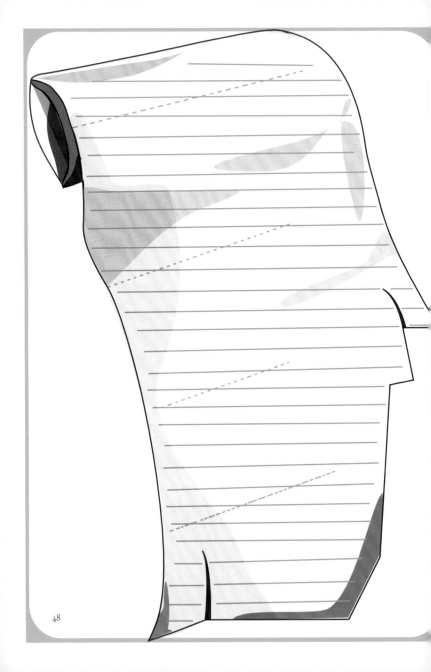

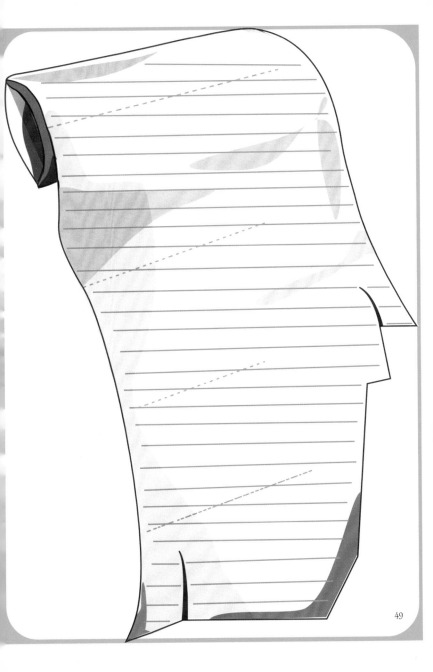

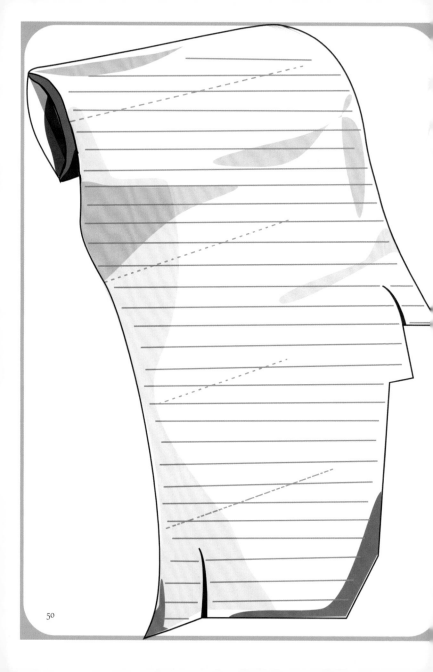

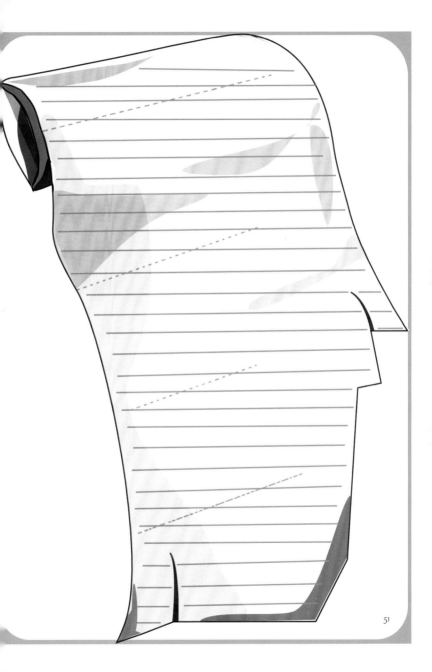

Acknowledgements:

I am so incredibly grateful to all of the people in my life. First and foremost, I thank my Parents Steve and Cindy for always supporting me to be creative and to pursue my dreams. I am so grateful for parents who have supported me in EVERYTHING that I've pursued in my life. I also thank you for teaching me to have a voice and that it's okay to use it. I thank you for showing me that no matter what has happened to you or what limitations you may have, you can achieve literally anything. Also, thanks for putting up with me during the shittier part of my teenage ye

I thank my brother Steven who, before I was aware of how to, blocked poop from coming at me and rescued me from the shitty situations that I stupidly got myself into. I cannot thank Steven without also thank my, Brother from another Mother, John who basically became an extension of my Bio bro. Thanks John! I thank my sister, Tera who has always promoted me to be a strong, independent, and take no-shit women! I also want to thank my extended family, aunts, uncles, and selects cousins, for being great influences on my life.

Thank you to all of my wild and crazy friends! You all have accepted me for who I am, and after the public reads this book they will realize that this is A LOT! I love you all for supporting me and laughing through the first drafts of this book. A special shout out to my besties Angel, Erika (and Dylan), Adrianne, Jessica, Melissa, and Amber who have LET ME hand them my poop, SEVERAL times, and still befriended me afterward. I'm sure we're all glad I am out of that phase.

I want to also thank my mentors, Kristi and Johnetta. You are both the most beautiful Angels and I thank you every day for giving me the motivation to keep going. I thank you both for your guidance and strength. While you are no longer on this earth, you are always in my heart and my head. Also a big thanks to my Publishing Coach Janine, Editor Kerri, and Bad-Ass graphic designer, Brenna.

I am so grateful for my amazing husband Mark who has supported me with all of my crazy goals, life changes, and for everything else crazy about me. I love you so much and I am so lucky to have such a loving, thoughtful, and supportive you! I cannot imagine pursuing this world with anyone but you. Your strength, patience, and intellect inspire me everyday. I am so thankful we found each other. You're also SMOKING hot!

I am also so grateful for my extended family in-laws for treating me as if I was one of your own! Love you guys!

To all of my nieces and nephews, I hope that this book inspires you to go towards your hopes and your dreams. To always remember to listen to yourself and recognize how to stay in control even when everything is falling apart around you!

Also a shout out to my fur-babies for always, no matter what, making sure their paws were on my keyboard while writing this book.

I thank all of my therapy clients and their families for allowing me to be creative in therapy sessions and trusting that this was best for your child. I know that at times I asked you to do and say off the wall things like, "that's your poop!" and I appreciate you humoring me!

Lastly, I want to thank everyone who has contributed to my life in both good and bad ways. We all have our story and those stories contribute to the people we become. I am thankful to have come out on top even with barriers (and bad choices) that got in my way. This is a testament to everyone out there that NO MATTER what happens to you, no matter the actions you chose or not chose to take, you can always find your best self. All it takes is realization that the emotional poo that was projected onto you was the pressure and influence of someone else in your life. It is not your truth. Your truth lies within you and when you can find YOUR actual voice, your truth will be loud and clear.

-C.J.H

About C.J. Hathaway, MAS, MFT

C.J. Hathaway is a marriage and family therapist turned author, speaker, life coach, and overall badass. C.J's work includes working as an advocate and clinician for children and young adults specializing in trauma, abuse, and eating disorders. C.J's work included working with local police, children's hospitals, and child welfare within C.J's state's child advocacy centers helping children to heal from trauma.

C.J. can be heard on several podcasts and newscasts including KTAR "Eyes on Parenting" and "The Mother's" podcast. C.J.'s passions include speaking at events that inspire others and promoting using their voice even when it makes people uncomfortable.

C.J. was born in California and cherishes her exposure to different cultures, views, and personalities throughout her life. C.J. spent the majority of early life within the creative arts, which helped C.J. find her passion and ability to express herself. She, being the persistent shit that she is, had hefty life goals, one being the first person in her immediate family to graduate from a four Year University and then receive a Postgraduate Degree in Marriage and Family Therapy.

If you can't tell her type of therapy is off the cuff and more down to earth than most. She has been described as "Constructively blunt with a side of sweet empowerment." Even within sessions she was known to curse, rap, and make up dumb examples to help her clients understand tools and concepts. This is where the phrase, "Don't Hold their Poop" and other poop references were born. Her goal was for her clients to leave therapy sessions remembering the shenanigans that came out of her mouth when they were triggered or in stressful situations. Per her client's account, it worked.

After her work with trauma victims, she decided to take a break from mental health work. She made a complete career change but always felt a need to continue helping people find their voice. She caved and decided to start her own Life Coaching Practice to help mentally well people find their best lives. She has helped several Professionals understand the poop they are bringing into romantic relationships that continually influenced shitty outcomes. Hmmm, spin off?

She has been with her husband for over six years and is childless by choice. She is a dog fanatic and if it was up to her, she would have a small dog gang. She enjoys donating her time to the less fortunate as well as promoting equality for all human beings and animals.

She hopes that you do not take yourself and your life too seriously. It's all a big bowel movement. Your choice is to settle and wipe with one ply or know your worth and flushable wet wipe that, literal, shit.

Contact the Author:
C.J. Hathaway, MAS, MFT
thatsnotmypoop@gmail.com
Instagram: @Thatsnotmypoop
Website: www.thatsnotmypoop.com